if

i

already

have

nothing

if
i
already
have
nothing

alana kirby

THE OUTSIDER **POET PRESS**

trigger warning

some of these poems contain topics related to:

abuse

death

sexual assault

eating disorders

suicide

when

love

isn't

enough

i appreciate your honesty even though it hurts. because when you say that it's over, i know you really mean it. i know there's nothing i can do to stop you from leaving.

but i'll still cry. i'll still wrap my arms around your leg like a child who's afraid to be left alone. it hurts just the same to hear the truth, if not even more.

sometimes i wish you'd lie. tell me you still love me and that it'll be okay. ***i'd rather hear you say you want me and not mean it than watch you walk away.***

"i love you"
i would give anything to hear you say
those words again. because i remember
the way you used to say them with such
certainty in your voice. like i was the
only girl in the world for you. like i was
your everything.

you promised that you'd love me
forever. until the stars no longer shined
in the night sky and the sun didn't rise
anymore. you promised that you'd stay.

you promised.
you promised.
you promised.

so tell me, why am i alone?

do you miss me when you're alone?
does every thought that you told
yourself no longer mattered suddenly
mean everything?

i hope my absence hurts you.
it's the least you deserve after
everything you did.

i just wanted you to love me.
**even though some part of me
always felt like i didn't deserve it.**

i always wonder if you regret what you
did to me. if the hands on the clock
could turn back far enough to bring me
back to you, would you take the risk of
loving me again?
sometimes i think you wish you could
fill the space between us. maybe it's
just wishful thinking. but i truly believe
you wanted things to be different.

i hope you regret what you did to me.
that if the hands on the clock could
turn back far enough to bring me back
to you, you would take the risk of loving
me again.
i hope deep down that you want to fill
the space between us. that it's not just
wishful thinking. i hope this time you
wouldn't love me the same. **but
instead, you'd do it the right way.**

in another lifetime, another world or
universe, we're together.
and we're so in love that it's as though
nothing else matters.

it's just us. it always has been.

i promise to never stop loving you no
matter what. i promise to always find
you no matter how much it hurts.

i don't know why. i just know that
i need you. and that i've never loved
someone with so much of my being
before.

i keep on dreaming of the day where
i can be with you even though i know
it may never come to be.

because what else can i do?

even if i found another to fill the empty
space, even if i tried to let go, my heart
would still beat for you.
it always has and it always will.

so maybe that's just the way it is.
maybe i was destined to love you.

i'd be lost without you.
you give me everything. so much
more than the rest of the world could.
i want to wrap you up in my arms and
hold you. i want to feel the way your
chest rises and falls when you breathe.
i'll always love you. **even when you**
stop loving me too.

i lost myself when you left.
it was the only way i could forget
about you.

i tried to ignore how i felt.
i tried to ignore how much i missed
you. but it never worked.

you still had all of me. you were still
the only person who mattered.

that was when i realized i couldn't
keep pretending anymore.
*that was when i realized i'd never
be able to let go of you.*

i always think of what we could've
been if things had been different.
i used to imagine spending the rest of
my life with you. i used to dream of us
having everything.
we'd get married someday and move
to the middle of nowhere. we'd spend
our evenings dancing around the
kitchen and laughing until we couldn't
breathe.
somedays the world can seem so cruel.
somedays it makes me feel completely
alone. but then i'm there with you.
and i feel at home. i feel so free.
i wish you were here with me. i wish
you missed me too. *because i know
that no matter what happens, my
heart will always wander back to
you.*

it's been a few years since the last time
i saw you.

every now and then, i wait by the door
and hope that you'll show up.

i hope you'll ring the doorbell.
i hope you'll sit on my doorstep as you
patiently wait for my arrival.

and most of all, i hope you'll smile with
the same light in your eyes that you had
when we first met.

i know that you won't.
i know it's really over.

but i can't let you go.

and if that's the case,
then i'll learn to accept it.

i don't know how.

**but someday i'll be okay in knowing
that you're gone.**

you were everything i wanted.
i know you never noticed. but i still
would've done anything to show you.
because no matter how much you
tried to shut me out, i couldn't let
you go. there was always some part
of me that missed you. the way
i felt wasn't something that could
just go away. i couldn't stop myself
from loving you.

i can't help but wonder why i wasn't
enough. *because i would've done
anything to be deserving of your love.*

i was so naive, thinking a heart like
yours could love a girl like me.
i needed you. my eyes couldn't see the
darkness beginning to consume me.
and before i knew it, it was too late.
you had already entangled me into your
being and i didn't know how to let go.

so why did you do it? why did you
betray me? maybe it wasn't enough for
you to build everything we had on a lie.
to tell me i was everything you had ever
wanted when it could've never been
true. *i could've never been enough
for you.*

i was so lost in you that i didn't even
care how much pain i was in. chasing
after you became a second instinct.
it felt like i needed you. your laughter
was the only medicine i wanted to take
and your smile made me forget how
much you were breaking me.
it was lonely. ***loving you was so
unbelievably lonely.***

will you ever come back?
maybe.
i don't know.

but i know that even if you did, things
would never be the same. i would never
be able to forgive you for what you did.
the way you pulled me up to heaven
and then threw me back down to hell
only to say *"climb your way out of it"*
and then when i couldn't, you left me
with nothing.

but darling, i'll still love you forever. in
the same way that you once promised
you did. ***the only difference this time is
that i won't let you know it.***

the truth is that i hate everyone but
you. i wouldn't mind watching the
world fall to its feet. i wouldn't mind
losing everything i've ever known.
in fact, i hope everything fades into
nothing. because as long as i have you,
i don't mind the pain.

you're all that matters to me. you're
all that ever will. even when the stars
stop shining and the world stops
spinning, i'll hold onto you. even when
i have nothing left but the emptiness
inside my soul and a head full of fear,
i'll still love you. because you mean
everything to me. ***you just do.***

i don't know if i'll ever be able to
forget you. our memories still sit in
the back of my mind like my old
favorite dress that doesn't fit
anymore. i can't put them back on
even though i'll always miss who
i was when i could.

because you moved on like it was
the easiest thing you had ever done.
you never even looked back or
questioned if it was the right thing
to do. so i can't help but wonder if
i deserved it.

i'm afraid i'll never be able to forget
you. *i'm afraid i'll never be able
to move on too.*

i hated you. i hated you for leaving and
i hated you for staying. i hated you for
everything you did to me because you
knew i didn't deserve it. you knew how
much it hurts to place your already
broken heart in the hands of someone
who has no intention of keeping it.
it felt like a piece of me died when you
left and it hurt even worse when you
came back just to stop me from letting
go of you. ***nothing has ever hurt
worse than loving you.***

you always said i was just like you.
it was your favorite thing about me.
maybe it was the way i played the role
of the perfect girl or that i never knew
how to say no.

you made me feel so small. it was like
i was crushed beneath the weight of
your approval. nothing i did was ever
enough.

i wanted so badly for you to care.
i wanted a reason or to somehow
understand why.

i wanted to let you go. *it's just hard to
let something go when it never stops
holding onto you.*

i'm sorry for everything.
you never deserved to break
because of me.
i should've been there for you.
i should've told you how much you
mattered to me or given you more.
instead, i let you down.
i know i can never make it up to you.
i can't pull the stars back into your
sky and i can't change what i did.
but i hope you know that i'm sorry.
i always will be.

i always knew you'd leave me
someday.
once the storm in my heart became
too much to handle.
once the wind in our sails became
impossible to swim against.
but i swear i loved you more than
i had ever loved anyone before.
i swear that it's true.
**i would've never left your side or
given up on you.**

you're everything i want.

you're the only thing that matters
anymore.

i've spent my entire life searching for an
answer to my pain.

some part of me always hoped none
of it was true.

but nothing hurts anymore.

at least, it doesn't when i'm with you.

when you touched me, it was more
than just a feeling of lust. the way your
fingertips traced up and down my chest
and your body collided with mine was
a different type of heaven. it made me
feel even closer to you. that was the
reason i craved it. i needed all of you.
***and i needed you to know that you
had all of me.***

i used to be heartbroken over you.
you destroyed me in so many ways.
it was hard to let it go.
all i ever wanted was for you to love
me. i wanted to be the girl you always
dreamed of. the one who held your
hand and chased away all your pain.
but i couldn't. i was too lost in the
waves of darkness that swallowed me
whole and the feeling of not being
enough. i couldn't be who you needed
me to be. ***and for that, i'm sorry.***

i watch you settle into the driver's seat.
you seem to feel at home in it. so i let
you stay.

it was actually a relief at first. i was so
tired from all the years i spent
navigating the busy streets. feeling
paralyzed by all the things that might
go wrong. i was desperate to let go of
control. and i had never felt as alive as
i did with you. it was beautiful to finally
understand hope. to finally be free.

but i should've never let you in.

all the magic we had surely died.
and there came a day where the door
opened again. because you never loved
me. you loved the feeling of knowing
i was yours. it hurts because even after
all this time, *i still am.* a part of me will
always belong to you. the part of me
you drove away with.

so now i wait by the curb, hoping you'll
return someday to give it back. you're
still in the driver's seat. ***i'm just not
there to hold you anymore.***

i felt nothing but sadness for you.
how could i not? i watched the way you
ached for someone to care and the way
your loneliness became a part of you.
i watched the way you cried with your
head buried in your pillowcase and the
way it so effortlessly drowned out the
sound. you seemed so broken. i never
understood why. but i know that
i loved you. ***and that i would've given
anything to make you feel whole
again.***

i loved her. the truth is that i always
knew i did. but it took me a long time
to understand why.

and it's funny because now that
i notice it, i don't know how i didn't
notice it before.

there was never a moment where
i didn't think of her. her laughter
always felt like home and her arms
were the only place i had ever
belonged. she was everything i didn't
know i needed.

but i never knew how to tell her.
i didn't even know where to begin.
***perhaps that's the reason why i'll
never know what we could've been.***

every time you ask *"do you really love me?"* i have to stop myself from telling you how much it hurts me.
because how could i not love you?
how could anyone look at you and say they didn't see your light?
you're the most beautiful soul in this world. there's no one else that makes me feel this way.
nothing terrifies me more than the thought of losing you.
so even though i build walls around my heart to ignore the pain, ***that's never enough to make how much i love you go away.***

i learned to hate everything about
myself because of you.
even the small things.
the things that are so insignificant
that no one else can notice them but
me.
from something as simple as the way
i hold my breath because i'm afraid
of anyone hearing me to the way
i changed everything about myself
to forget who i was. nothing ever
made me forget what you did.
and even though no one will ever
notice it or see, *i hate myself
because i'm afraid you'll always be
a part of me.*

i never told you how much i needed
you.
what we had was real even though
i swore it wasn't.
the life i had planned with you.
the way i would've done anything to
make you stay.
i wanted what we had to be true.
**i wanted it as long as it was with
you.**

you promised to stay.
maybe it was my fault for believing
you.
but i loved you so it was hard to not
have faith.

how can you blame me for trying?
you know i would've done anything to
make it work.
you know i would've done anything to
be enough.
**sometimes i wonder why you couldn't
see that i already was.**

i miss what life was like before you
left. i never understood what i did
to deserve it.
all i want is to wake up next to you.
for you to tell me it was all a dream.
that nothing could ever be enough
to take you away from me.

in the back of my mind, you're still
here with me. your voice plays on
repeat in my head and every time
i hear it, i can't help but give into
you again.

i don't have the choice to forget you
even though it's all i want.
it's like no matter how much i try to
move on, i still never can. *it's like no
matter what i do, everything comes
back to you.*

you used to make me feel so loved.
but lately, all i feel is emptiness in
place of where you should be.
i always wonder what i did to make
you shut me out. sometimes i wonder
if it was even my fault.
because you never told me the reason
why. you just left like i was nothing.

but even after all this time, i still love
you the same. i still miss you and
i still need you.

i hope you come back someday. you
mean more to me than you'll ever
know. *that's why i promise to never
let you go.*

i'll never love someone again because
of you. because even if i did, it wouldn't
be the same. i know my heart will
always belong to you. i've learned to
accept that you're a part of me.
it just hurts because i never expected
you to leave. i thought that even if
you did, you'd somehow find your
way back to me.

it's been so long that i can barely
remember the sound of your voice or
how it felt when you held me. i can
barely remember the reason why
i ever needed you at all or why you
meant so much to me.
i can barely remember you. *i can just
remember that i loved you.*

loving you was never the part that
hurt. loving you was the most
beautiful thing i had ever done.
because you were the answer to
everything. you were the light that
showed me a way when i couldn't
remember where i was. you were
the part of me that hung onto hope
no matter how hard things got.
i wanted you to love me as much as
i loved you. i never understood why
you couldn't.

loving you was never the part that
hurt. loving you was the easiest
thing i had ever done.
because you were all i wanted.
i pulled the stars out of my sky just
to make you stay. i abandoned
every single part of myself just so
you wouldn't.
i wanted you to love me as much as
i loved you. *i understand now that
you couldn't.*

i thought i'd never let go of you.
i thought i'd miss you forever like the
moon misses the sun. that i'd never
stop hearing your laughter or the way
you whispered *"i love you"* because
i wasn't just sad. i was completely
broken. losing you felt like the end of
everything. your absence left a hole in
my chest, an emptiness that i could
only hopelessly try to fill. i was ready to
accept that you were a part of me.

but then there came a day where the
sun finally showed again. the stars
shined a little brighter and the
emptiness didn't feel so heavy.
i stopped hearing your laughter and
seeing you down the empty hallway.
i wasn't broken anymore. i used to
think losing you was the end of
everything. that i'd feel the pain of it
forever. but then there came a day
where i was okay. ***there came a day
where i didn't need you anymore.***

teach

me

how

to

let

go

the feeling of being insignificant is one
that's existed in me for as long as i can
remember. like a star that only shines in
the morning sky, you would never
notice me next to the beauty of the sun.

i want someone to see me. not just the
surface. but all of me. all of my
madness and beauty. all of my darkness
and light. i want someone to dance with
me. hold me in their arms and tell
i'm enough. *for i've never quite
understood how it feels to be loved.*

i toss my clothes in the washing
machine for what feels like the
millionth time. they're filthy just like
me. they haven't been much else since
what you did.
i keep on washing them. over and over
again. pouring chemicals into the water
to try and remove the dirt. scrubbing at
the stain until it's so insignificant that
no one else can notice it but me.
and i notice it. i notice it every single
moment that i'm awake. and every time
i notice it, i remember you. how you
threw me on the ground while
i screamed for you to stop. how you
held me there and forced me to take it.
you never heard me, did you? you
wouldn't have listened either way.
but it's just dirt. it's nothing more than
a stain. ***i'm just forced to wear what
you did to me for the rest of my life.***

i'm tired of myself. there's nothing
more to it. i want to rip myself out of
my body and watch it waste away.
i want to see the way it struggles to
hold on to its being only to eventually
give up anyway. i don't want to think
anymore. i don't want to be. it's almost
unbearable. i feel sick from the broken
feeling inside my heart despite the fact
that i can barely feel anything at all.
i feel sick because there's nothing i can
do to change it. and i wonder how
that's possible. ***how i can feel nothing
and everything at once.***

i do everything i can to make myself forget about you. i scream your name into my pillowcase every night in hopes that if i repeat what you did enough times, i won't remember it anymore. i dress in baggy clothing so that it's harder for someone else to take the body that shamefully exists beneath them. i pray and i pray that i'll stop thinking of how you touched my skin despite the way it screamed for you to stop. but i never do. ***i never stop thinking of you.***

i see the way you lay awake at night,
staring at your ceiling and just wishing
you could waste away. it hurts, doesn't
it? it hurts even worse because no one
understands it.

they tell you that it's hopeless.
that nothing could ever be enough to
mend the hole inside your heart.

so you believe them. and you learn to
give up on yourself because everyone
else did.

yet i know you deserve more than that.
i see the light that shines from within
you despite the miles of darkness that
consume your being. you're so much
more than what you've been told.

even though you might never believe
me or think it's true, ***i'm so proud of
you for continuing to fight because
i know how much you don't want to.***

you have permission to feel. to smile
and laugh but also cry and fall apart.
it doesn't make you weak to exist as
you are. *even when the world insists
it's wrong to live from your heart.*

i dreamed of being the girl that people couldn't ignore. the one people turned their heads to look at when she walked by. i wanted more than anything to be beautiful and i envied the women who effortlessly wore perfection like it was as easy as putting on a pair of clothes. aphrodite would've been proud of them. they were so full of beauty and grace. so completely breathtaking. and i was as nothing as a girl could be. i broke my soul trying to place myself into their world despite the fact that i knew i didn't belong in it. every time i looked in the mirror, i couldn't help but attempt to tear my heart out to ease the pain of what i saw. i wasn't enough on the surface or from what only the eyes could see. ***and i always knew that beautiful was just something i was never meant to be.***

i remember the moment i arrived at
your funeral. i dressed in all black like
they had told me to. i guess i didn't
realize that after the suffering,
everyone would return to their
normal states. they would continue
to walk around in their white clothes
and pretend like you never existed.

but i couldn't be like everyone else.
even as time went on, the image of
rain pouring down on your casket
lived in my head and your laughter
still followed me everywhere i went.
because even though you were gone,
your ghost became a part of me.
it would sometimes wrap me up in its
arms and hold me while i was lost in the
dark, whispering for me to let you go.
**and darling, the truth is that i never
could.**

*"why do you try so hard to shut the
world out?"* i whispered to her.

she was so beautiful. so amazing in all
that she did. everyone knew it too.
from the way her smile made the world
seem whole again to the way she put
the broken pieces of my soul back
together. i didn't understand how
someone like her could believe she
wasn't enough.

"because nobody sees me" she
whispered back. *"they see the girl that
i pretend to be"*

and suddenly, i knew what she meant.

all those nights she spent alone,
screaming at the mirror because she
couldn't stand what she saw. all those
times she held onto me, hoping that if
she got close enough, it would turn her
into someone else. she learned to shut
the world out because it had broken her
heart. nobody had ever seen the person
underneath her mask and still fallen in
love with her. so she forced herself to
change. **and she made it so that
everyone who fell in love with her, fell
in love with a version of her that didn't
exist.**

i didn't understand what the world
was like as a child. i think i always
understood what my world was
supposed to be. but it never lined up
with what happened to me.
i wasn't fed my childhood on a spoon
with the taste of pink princess blankets
and sugar. i didn't see the days where
the sun should've been stronger than
the rain and the sweet sound of
innocence should've consumed me.
i only ever had the darkness. and
i thought that meant there was
something wrong with me.
i always thought that maybe if i had
told you to stop a little bit louder,
you wouldn't have assaulted me.
that maybe it was my fault for not
being okay with what you did.

i only ever wanted to save us.
you were supposed to be the person
who stood by my side no matter
what life put us through.
so no matter how much it broke my
heart to be helpless to the way you
stole my innocence and made my
body your own, *it was always the
pain of losing you that hurt the most.*

recovery was never a linear path for
me. there were nights where i stayed
up crying because i couldn't stand to
face my own reflection. there were days
where i felt like i couldn't breathe
because my grief was suffocating me.
it was never easy. it forced me to break.
but i kept fighting to get better. *in the
end, that was all that really mattered.*

this is to you, the broken girl i call my
home. i know we haven't spoken in
what feels like an eternity. i wish
i could give you a better reason why.

i'm sorry that i wasn't there to hold
you through your pain. the truth is that
i didn't know how to. you always
seemed at home in it. like you didn't
want it to go away.
i know now more than ever how much
you needed me. *i know now more
than ever how much i hurt you.*

no matter if i'm surrounded by people
who love me or if i'm completely alone,
i feel just as alone inside because no
one knows who i am behind the person
i pretend to be.

nothing hurts me worse than having to
go through life being a stranger to
everyone i know.

i'm always alone. i'm alone when
i wake up and i'm alone when i go to
sleep. i'm alone because all i do is hide.

i barely feel like a person anymore.
it's like everything i'm doing is an
attempt to push down the truth.
*it's like no matter how much i try to
forget myself, i still never do.*

i miss myself.
there's nothing more to it.

every time i'm alone, i'm reminded
of her absence. she continues to
hold onto me while begging me to
let her go.

and it hurts. it hurts because there's
nothing i can do to make her
understand how much i need her.

she's the answer to all of my pain.
she's the only person i'll ever need.
i just can't love another without
wishing she was there instead.

but i keep screaming at the girl in the
mirror, the same one who carries the
weight of my broken soul. *i hate her*
because i'll never understand how
it feels to be whole.

i've come to learn it's easier to accept
my pain than to pretend it doesn't
exist. but i still can't help the urge to
run.

all i ever wanted was to be loved.
**that's why it hurts that i wasn't
enough.**

it hurts when you're taught to be
someone you're not. when you're
taught you aren't deserving of love
if you're different.
i hope there's more to who i am
than what i've been told. because
i miss myself more than anything
in the world.

i miss the way i used to smile at
even the smallest of things. before
the world broke me, i held so much
love for everything.
i miss the way i used to laugh until
i couldn't breathe. before i lost
myself, heartbreak wasn't a burden
i had ever known.
and even though i've spent all this
time running away, trying so hard
to be someone else, *the only
person i wish i could be with
anymore is myself.*

no one understood how to accept me.
it broke my heart because all i wanted
was for someone to see me. i wanted
to be told i was enough.

i didn't understand how to accept
myself. it broke my heart because
i couldn't face the truth of who i was.
i never knew how to let anyone in.
i only knew how to pretend that i did.

my father was alone and his heart was
broken from the rejection the world put
him through.
he faked a smile even when it was so
obvious that all he wanted to do was
cry.
his heart was his greatest strength yet
also his greatest fear. nobody
understood him because he didn't
know how to let anyone in.
but i understand now that he was afraid
of how much he felt. just like me.

my mother was ignored and her heart
was broken from always hearing
nothing but her own echo.
she faked rage even when it was so
obvious that all she wanted to do was
ask *"why does nobody hear me?"*
her voice was her greatest strength yet
also her greatest fear. nobody heard
her because she used anger instead
of all the love she so beautifully had
to give.
but i can hear now that she was afraid
of never being enough. ***just like me.***

i'm afraid of my own heart. i'm afraid
of how much it feels. i'm afraid of the
way it aches to love so deeply that it
never stops overflowing with a light
so bright that it's enough to guide
even the darkest of nights home.

because i don't understand it.
i don't understand why i feel so
much. i was always told it was easier
to walk through life without the
needlessness of compassion. and yet,
i can't let go of it no matter how
hard i try.

i know that even when i deny the
truth, it's still there. i know that
even when i tell myself i don't care,
i always do.
***so if i'm telling the truth, all i want
is to love and to be loved too.***

i'm tired of losing myself over and over
again. i'm starting to think i have
nothing left.

if things never get better then what do
i do? *if i always feel this way then is it
my fault for telling myself to?*

your mind can't get rid of your heart.
*it can only manipulate your heart
into thinking that it did.*

as a kid, people used to tell me that
getting older meant letting go of
the things you love. they said i'd
understand one day what life is truly
like.

so i stopped doing the things i loved.
i stopped taking bubble baths and
playing with toys. i stopped watching
my favorite tv show.
i used to admire sunsets and all of the
good things about life. so i can't help
but wonder why i have nothing
anymore.

they told me that growing up meant
letting go of the things i loved. *they*
told me that growing up meant not
being happy anymore.

i wish i had loved myself better.
she deserved so much more than
what i had to give.
it must hurt being so beautiful but
only ever being told you're too much
by a world that doesn't understand
how to accept you.

there's nothing wrong with her.
i had to learn the hard way that just
because you can't understand
something doesn't mean it deserves
to be ignored.

i regret being afraid of her darkness.
i didn't realize that the stars could
offer just as much as the sun.
i miss her and i hope she knows
i regret breaking her too.

i think it's beautiful how you continue to hold so much love in your heart despite losing everything you've ever known. *to me, there's nothing more beautiful than that.*

depression is a disease. maybe you can't see it. but that doesn't mean it isn't there. that doesn't mean it'll somehow find a way to stop holding onto you.

you see, depression will do everything in its power to kill you. it's the voice in your head that tells you it's easier to close the curtains and go back to bed because waking up means having to face your own emptiness.

it's the voice in your head that tells you no one will miss you when your pain becomes too much and you can't carry on anymore.

it'll split you in half and still somehow leave you with nothing. *and in the end, all you'll want is to finally feel something.*

the problem is that i'm scared to be
touched. i'm like a rose that's had its
thorns up its entire life so that no one
notices the way i ache to love
underneath my pain.
because despite how scared i am of
being touched, it's all i've ever wanted.
i want someone to prick themselves
on my thorns and still be desperate
for more. i know i don't deserve it.
i want someone to bleed all over me
from the sting of my touch and still
say they understand that isn't the
real me. i know i'm not easy to love.
but i hope someday that someone
will see how much i ache to love
underneath my pain. *i hope that'll
be the reason they decide to be
the first person who ever stayed.*

no one had ever loved me before.
people loved me for who they thought
i could be.
on the surface, i faked a smile.
i laughed and told everyone it was okay.
they wanted to believe they knew me.
but none of them ever did.

i had never loved myself before.
i loved myself for who i thought i could
be.
i knew how to fake a smile. i knew how
to laugh and tell myself it was okay.
i wanted to believe i knew me.
but deep down, i never did.

"i've been lost for as long as i can remember" i told myself.
"and why do you think that is?" she responded.
"i don't know. but it's like even when i have everything, i still have nothing" i said.
"the reason for that is because you don't have me" she insisted.

and i know she's right. i just don't know what to do. despite the emptiness that's become a part of me, i still return to everything but the one who could fix it. i love her even though i hate her. i miss her even though i'm the one who abandoned her.

"you're wrong. i don't need you" i screamed.
"i'll always wait for you even though it hurts" she whispered back to me.

true happiness comes from the
art of having love for everything
**without feeling like you need
anything to be fulfilled.**

i used to think my emptiness had
nothing to offer me and because
of this, i was afraid for the longest
time.
i thought i was broken. i thought
i was lost and would never find
a single reason to believe again.
because i saw i was in pain and
i ran away from myself the same
way everyone else had.
"i'm too much" i told myself the
reason was. i've always been just
a little bit too much. too much
for the world. too much for
everyone. too much for me.

but despite how much i swore
this was true, i still couldn't push
myself away. i still found myself
on my front porch each night,
i still heard myself banging on the
door, screaming *"i'm still here
even if you don't let me in"*
and i never figured out how to
let her in. i was afraid for the
longest time of what i'd see.
**now my house is abandoned and
she's trying to open a door that
no longer has a key.**

i've secretly always been soft. but
i never wanted people to know this.
i hid behind a mask built on lies and
machiavellianism because i was afraid
of who i was inside.
on the surface, i felt nothing. the world
hated me for being so cold but i knew
they'd hate the vulnerability inside me
more. so i shut myself out so that no
one could steal away my light.
i knew leaving myself meant i'd always
feel like something was missing but
i knew it'd hurt more to be myself in a
society that wasn't built for accepting
people like me.

abandoning myself destroyed me. for
the longest time, it was the worst and
only pain i'd ever known.
but eventually the pain became so
much that all i could feel anymore was
emptiness.

"something's missing" a voice inside me
screamed.
"something's missing" i hate who
i pretended to be.
"something's missing" **the answer has
always been me.**

and suddenly, everything changed. even
in this room full of strangers whispering
things they thought they knew about
me *(of course, they never really knew)*
i wasn't afraid anymore. it didn't matter
what anyone could possibly say. it
didn't matter that in my head they were
all drowning me, screaming at me,
telling me it was my fault for not being
who they wanted.
and suddenly, i didn't hear any of them
anymore. all i heard was a voice from
within saying *"i accept you. i love you
even though no one else saw any
reason to"*
and suddenly, i was okay.

what

i've

been

missing

i don't care about playing it cool.
maybe that makes me foolish or wrong.
it doesn't matter either way.

i'll shout it from the rooftops. i'll shout
it loud enough for everyone to hear.
i'm not afraid to say that i love you.

i love her body. i love her face. *i'm in love with the way she looks.* she could capture my heart with nothing more than a smile. the way her body curves and the wind blows in her hair. she takes my breath away. she's the most beautiful girl i've ever seen.

i love her heart. i love her laughter. *i'm in love with who she is.* she could capture my heart with nothing more than her light. the way she speaks of hope and makes even the worst of days feel okay. she takes my breath away. **she's the most beautiful girl i've ever known.**

you looked beautiful. you always do.
i watched with your hand on the
window sill and the wind in your face.
you laughed as the night sky fell in
love with the stars that danced upon it.
the thunder roared proudly and the
lightning flashed on without end.
it felt as if it'd last forever.
but you smiled at the storm.
in fact, you almost seemed to
welcome it. i know that's something
you'd probably do. because you're
wondrous like that. you could stare
darkness right in the eye and tell it how
much light you see in it. you could bring
comfort to even the loneliest of worlds.
it's no wonder you're everything to me.

i fell in love with everything about her.
it was more than just the way she made
me feel. or the way she looked. it was
the way she set the world on fire when
it was nothing but darkness. the way
her smile created a symphony of love
inside my broken heart. she was the
most amazing girl i'd ever met. i didn't
know how she did it. how she could
possibly bring hope to even the most
hopeless of people. how she could
reignite the fire inside my heart. *and
still,* she doesn't believe me when i tell
her how special she is. i know she
probably never will. *but even then,*
i'll remind her everyday how beautiful
she is. just how much she glows. ***i love
her more than she'll ever know.***

we sat in the driveway that night.
the skyline was painted different shades
of orange and pink. the summer air had
never felt so comforting. birds singing
and the smell of firewood burning.
kids laughing and riding their bikes in
the middle of the street. this was all
i had ever wanted. and yet, i just kept
staring at you. you eventually noticed.
you always do.
you put your arms around my shoulders
and gave me a smile. the same smile
that reminded me how important it is
to believe. and i just remember thinking
to myself "***how is it that even in all
this beauty, you're the only thing
i want to see?***"

i didn't know that you were what i was
searching for all along. i never much
believed in love.

but when i look at you, i see everything
we could be. i see early christmas
mornings and our children opening
presents. i see us driving around
town at midnight with our
windows rolled down and the music
turned all the way up.

you're all that matters to me and
sometimes it makes me so sad.
**because when i look at you, i see a life
full of all the things i never thought
i'd have.**

when you're with me, i'm free.
nothing seems to scare me anymore.
your love gives me so much strength.

i used to be so afraid to love, to fall.
***but now i know that if it isn't you
then it's no one at all.***

i want to have you. i want to hold you in my arms and tell you how much you matter. because you deserve it. you're my shooting star in even the darkest of nights. you're worth more than the world.

i was never one for falling in love. i was never one to believe in fairytales and happily ever afters. but then i met you. *i just can't deny how much i love you.*

she crept into my heart. the way she
laughed and danced. the way she fell
into my arms. she brought me back to
life. this world had made me feel like
i was cursed to be alone. to spend a
lifetime chasing after some
resemblance of closure that would
never come to be. it was tiring feeling
this way. the days were dark and
lonely. my hope was beginning to fade.
and then i saw her. i held her. and it
was as though my walls could no
longer pretend. *it was as though the
world was whole again.*

i know that i love you because
i'm content even when we're
surrounded by silence.
something about me is that
i've always hated the quiet.
i hate the way it makes me think.
how painfully loud the sound of
nothingness is.
but it's different when i'm with you.
i don't seem to crave the noise
anymore.
all i can think of is you.
the way your breathing slows.
how you effortlessly light up my
soul.
you bring me comfort without even
trying.
and i can't help but love you for that.

the reason i hold on is because i love
you. you never believe me when i tell
you. but i'll still say it anyway.
you're everything to me.
no. you're more than everything.
you're more than every sunrise.
you're more than the stars that light
up the sky and all of the beauty within
this broken world.
heaven on earth is only the beginning
of what you mean to me.
you could never be nothing.
you'll always be enough for me.

i needed you. i needed you more
than i'd ever needed anything before.
nothing could've stopped the way
i felt. ***nothing could've stopped me
from loving you.***

you make me smile. that's more
than anyone else can say.
you understand me. i don't have to
pretend to be someone else when
i'm with you. you love me the most
when i'm not even trying. it means
everything to me because i got so tired
of running away from myself.
you make me feel like i can finally
breathe. *you make me feel like there's
so much beauty beyond the darkness
that i've been too lost to see.*

you're the only person who knows my
heart. no one understands me the way
that you do.

there's so much i wish i could say. like
how i missed you and that i tried with
everything in me to forget you but
i still never could.

you're my home. you're the only thing
that matters anymore. i'm not afraid
of falling or losing what i used to know.
the life i had made for myself was
never what i truly wanted. it was no
wonder i felt so empty inside.

but you found me. you filled the
space inside my heart. *it's funny
because i always thought love was
meant to tear you apart.*

i'd make you see yourself the way i do
if i ever figured out how to. you always
say there's nothing beautiful about
you. but i know that could never be
true. because when i look at you, i see
everything i've ever wanted. you're
every dream of mine come true.
i just wish you knew you deserve all
of the things that you tell yourself
you don't.

i'll never stop loving you. your laughter
will never grow old and your smile
will always be the reason for mine.
how are you so beautiful without even
trying? tell me, how do you only
become more wondrous by the day?

i know you don't see yourself the way
i do. it's something i've learned to
accept. but everything you do takes my
breath away. *you're enough no matter
what you say.*

the morning sun shines through my
windows each morning to remind me
that the darkness has passed.
this simple act makes me think of you.

you taught me that it's okay to begin
again. to forget the pain of the past
and who i thought i was.
i want to hold onto you so tight that
i forget i even have the choice to let go.
because i know that i'd be broken
without you. that my heart would be
so sad. *i know that a life without you
is a life i don't ever want to have.*

you're breathtaking.
i'm in love with the way your eyes
shine in the sun and the sincerity
behind your smile. you made me
believe again.
there's nothing more precious than
your heart. it's filled with a light so
bright that even the darkness can't
help but stare.
and i always thought i was destined
to be alone. to be consumed by the
brokenness inside my own heart.
yet when you held me, i felt my
world change. i saw everything
i had ever known die before my eyes.
***what would i do without you in
my life?***

i was always told that heaven was
a place where girls like me weren't
allowed the privilege of being. but
then tell me, how do i have the
privilege of loving you?

your heart is the purest thing i've
ever felt and when you wrap your
arms around me, i know that i'm
home.

your love tastes like all of my worst
sins and i'm not afraid to say that
i don't regret any of them.

you're the most beautiful girl i've
ever known. you're worth more
than those who don't understand us.

because even though they say that
we're blind, i think they're the ones
who can't see. ***if loving you is hell
then i promise that heaven will
never be enough for me.***

i want you to hold me in your arms
and whisper every thought that comes
to your precious mind because your
voice will always be my favorite sound.
i want you to keep on repeating that
you love me until i believe it.

you make the world seem like it's
more than all of the loneliness i've felt.
that's why i'm not afraid of how much
i feel for you. i know that what we
have is real. i'll always love you.
and i know you'll always love me too.

i'm proud of you for still being here.
i see your pain. i would do anything
to take it away. because i know you
deserve so much more.

you don't realize how much you
mean to me. you don't understand
how much i wish you could.
**if there was a way to make you
see it, i promise you i would.**

i'll never forget the way you reached
for me just as i was about to hit the
ground. i'll never forget the way you
pulled me up and told me it wasn't
my fate to keep falling forever, that
there had to come a point where
i realized i deserved more.

and the truth is that i never knew
how you could think that. i didn't
understand why you thought i could
be anything more than my pain.
but you made me finally believe.
**you helped me find beauty in all
of the darkest parts of me.**

i hope you learn to love yourself
someday. and if you don't learn to
love then i hope you at least learn
to accept.
i know you don't think you deserve
it. everything you've been searching
for is already a part of you. you're
burdened by all the things you wish
you could be without realizing that
you already are.

and i'm proud of you. you're so
much stronger than you know.
you're still enough even on days
when all you can do is cry and lay
in bed.
**so if you never learn to love yourself
then i promise to love you instead.**

i wanted to forget you. i swear i tried
with everything in me to. but you
were never something that could be
forgotten. my heart has never ached
for someone quite as much as it does
for you.

love left me broken time and time
again. because of this, i was afraid to
feel. i had lost everything and i didn't
want things to get worse.
i promised myself i'd never love again.
but somehow there's not a single part
of me that regrets letting you in.

i hope you know that your beauty is
something i'll always see.
**i hope you know i love you in all the
ways that the world couldn't love me.**

i know that no one has ever loved you
before. maybe they tried to. maybe
they did everything they could and
maybe they even almost got it right.
but i know that no one has ever loved
you in the way you deserve.

you deserve a love so real that you
never have to question if it's right.
i never want you to think that you
aren't enough.
because it's not your fault they
didn't see your beauty. *it's their
fault for saying they couldn't see
while they had their eyes closed.*

if i ever had the privilege of touching
you, i think i'd lose myself in you for
the rest of forever.
there's something in your eyes when
you smile that makes me foolishly
believe you want me as much as
i want you.

can you feel the desperation inside
me doing everything not to break?
because i've never been one for love.
i always thought the lonely freedom
of needing no one was better than
eternally craving something i might
never be able to feel.

but i want to pick you apart piece by
piece. i want to know every inch of
your soul. i want to feel how much
you love me, and after that, i want
to feel even more.

i knew how to lose myself in my pain
so that i didn't have to face how much
i wanted to lose myself in you.
i knew how to pretend it was better
this way.
but all i ever wanted was to fall into
you. ***all i ever wanted was to love you.***

about

the

author

Alana Kirby is a teen poet from Baltimore, Maryland. She's enjoyed writing from the time she was a little girl but she didn't begin sharing her work online until she was 14 years old. Since doing this, she has gained a massive online following and inspired hundreds of thousands of people through her words. Her first book, *the words i'll never say*, became an Amazon poetry bestseller overnight and sold over 10,000 copies in its first six months. Helping others through her poetry has instilled a newfound sense of confidence in her passion for writing. She loves being a light to others and finds comfort in knowing others can relate to the emotions and life experiences she's been through.

TikTok: @outsiderpoetpress
Instagram: @outsiderpoetpress

if i already have nothing

ISBN (paperback): 978-1959373186
ISBN (ebook): 978-1959373018

The Outsider Poet Press, LLC
6405 Old Harford Road
Baltimore, MD 21214

Cover Design & Layout: Kairos Book Design